How to Make Cakes, Crumpets, Buns & Biscuits

by

Geoff Wells

Published by Geezer Guides

Copyright© 2012 Geoff Wells

ISBN-13: 978-1482592979

ISBN-10: 1482592975

~~~

License Notes

All rights reserved. No part of this book may be reproduced in any form by any electronic or mechanical means including photocopying, recording, or information storage and retrieval without permission in writing from the author.

http://www.authenticenglishrecipes.com/

Contents

Introduction 3
Bakewell Tarts 4
English Shortbread 6
Scones 8
Chelsea Buns 10
Chelsea Buns (Bread Machine Method) 13
Victoria Sponge Cake 15
Crumpets 17
Crumpets (Bread Machine Method) 20
Custard Tarts 22
Dundee Cake 24
English Bath Buns (Bread Machine Method) 26
English Muffins 28
English Muffins (Bread Machine Method) 31
Digestive Biscuits 33
Hot Cross Buns (Bread Machine Method) 35
Madeleines 38
Maid of Honour Tarts 40
Sausage Rolls 41
Pastry Tart Shells 42
International Measurement Equivalents 43
Please Review 46
About The Author 47

INTRODUCTION

Most of the books in this series are more about the method and ingredients of the recipes rather than exact quantities. This one is a little different as it is all about baking and baking just won't work unless you get the chemistry right.

These are my mother's recipes, modified for the North American measuring system. I have also changed any reference to self-raising flour because it is not widely available here.

I also want to thank my wife Vicky for developing the bread machine versions which will help to make these classic British favorites easier to make and therefore more available to busy cooks.

Bakewell Tarts

Bakewell tarts were one of my favorite treats growing up. The hard icing and the taste of the almond with the raspberry jam are sure to make these as popular in your family as they are in mine.

Ingredients

24 unbaked tart shells

Filling

½ cup butter
⅓ cup almond paste
½ cup sugar
3 eggs, slightly beaten
⅓ cup all purpose flour
1 cup raspberry jam

Icing

1 ⅓ cups confectioners sugar
2 tablespoons milk

Garnish

12 maraschino cherries, halved

Method

Pre-heat the oven to 400°F.

In a medium bowl, beat the butter with an electric mixer on low until creamy. Gradually add the almond paste and sugar and continue to beat on low speed until smooth. Add the eggs one at a time while continuing to beat on low speed. Fold in the flour just until it is well blended.

Spoon a heaping teaspoon of jam into each tart shell. Then spoon the filling into each shell, dividing it equally between all of the shells.

Bake the tarts in a 400°F oven for about 12 to 15 minutes, or until they are golden brown.

Remove from the oven and cool completely on a wire rack.

TO MAKE THE ICING

In a small bowl combine the confectioners sugar (icing sugar) with about 2 tablespoons of water and stir until smooth. Spoon the icing over the completely cooled tarts.

To garnish, place a maraschino cherry half in the middle of each tart and press slightly into the icing. Allow the icing to hardened slightly before serving.

SERVINGS: 24

ENGLISH SHORTBREAD

Store bought shortbread always seems so expensive for something so simple to make. Also by making it yourself you know it won't come with unwanted chemicals.

INGREDIENTS

    1 cup salted butter, DO NOT SUBSTITUTE MARGARINE
    ½ cup sugar
    3 cups all purpose flour

METHOD

Pre-heat the oven to 375°F.

Cream the butter and sugar together until light and fluffy.

Gradually mix in the flour using a fork and then your hands. The mixture may be a bit crumbly.

Firmly and evenly press the mixture into a 9 inch by 13 inch greased baking pan.

With a fork, prick the dough well, then lightly score the dough, with a very sharp knife, into bars.

Bake at 375°F for about 20 minutes or until it is a light golden brown.

Remove the shortbread from the oven and allow to cool completely on a wire rack.

When the shortbread has cooled completely, cut it into bars along the score lines.

SERVINGS: 12

SCONES

Serve these scones instead of bread for a delicious change of pace.

INGREDIENTS

    2 cups all purpose flour
    3 teaspoons baking powder
    ½ teaspoon salt
    2 tablespoons sugar
    ⅓ cup shortening
    2 large eggs, slightly beaten
    ½ cup whole milk or cream, approximately

METHOD

Pre-heat the oven to 425°F.

In a large bowl, combine the flour, baking powder, salt and sugar. Mix well.

Cut in the shortening with a pastry blender until the mixture resembles a coarse corn meal.

In a separate measuring cup, add enough milk to the slightly beaten eggs to make ¾ cup. Mix well.

While stirring with a fork, add just enough of the liquid to make a soft dough. Continue stirring until all of the flour disappears.

On a lightly floured surface, knead the dough for about 30 seconds.

Either pat the dough down, or roll it out, to about ½ inch thick.

Cut into rounds with a cookie cutter. You should get 10 to 12 scones.

You can re-use any scrap left over from cutting the dough by reforming and cutting again.

Note: Only do this once. After that the dough will become too tough and too dry.

Place the scones on a greased baking sheet and bake at 425°F for 12 to 15 minutes.

Serve warm.

SERVINGS: 12

Chelsea Buns

Chelsea buns look very much like cinnamon buns but the dough is very different. Chelsea buns are made with yeast and are like a sweet bread.

Ingredients

    1 cup milk, room temperature
    1 teaspoon salt
    2 eggs, room temperature
    2 tablespoons butter, softened
    3 cups all purpose flour
    1½ teaspoons yeast
    1½ cups dried mixed fruit, finely chopped
    ½ cup light brown sugar
    ½ teaspoon ground cinnamon
    ⅛ teaspoon ground nutmeg
    ⅛ teaspoon ground ginger
    ⅛ teaspoon ground allspice
    ⅛ teaspoon ground cloves
    ¼ cup butter, melted

Glaze
¼ cup superfine sugar
¼ cup milk

Method

Combine the flour and the salt in a large bowl. Create a depression in the middle of the flour and add the dried yeast.

In a small saucepan, heat the milk and butter together over medium heat until the butter melts and the mixture is lukewarm.

Add the milk mixture and the eggs to the flour mixture and stir until the mixture forms a soft dough.

Turn the dough out onto a well floured work surface and knead for about five minutes. Add more flour, if necessary, until the dough is smooth, elastic and no longer sticks to your hands.

Lightly oil a large bowl. Place the dough in the bowl and turn it so that the dough gets a light covering of oil. Cover the bowl with plastic wrap and let it stand in a warm area for about an hour. The dough should double in size.

Note: the best place for the dough to rise is in the oven with only the oven light turned on.

Punch down the dough and roll it out on a lightly floured surface to form a rectangle approximately 9 inches by 22 inches. Mix together the dried fruit, brown sugar and spices. Brush the dough with the melted butter and sprinkle with the fruit mixture. Roll up the dough, from the long side, into a Swiss roll shape and cut into 18 equal pieces using a very sharp knife.

Arrange the buns, cut side down, in a lightly buttered 9 inch by 13 inch baking pan. Lightly brush the tops of the buns with melted butter and cover with plastic wrap. Allow the buns to rise in a warm area for about 30-45 minutes. The buns should be touching each other and the dough will be springy.

Note: the ideal place for the buns to rise is in the oven with just the oven light on.

Before pre-heating the oven, remove the risen buns and, carefully, remove the plastic wrap. Then, pre-heat the oven to 375°F.

Bake at 375°F for about 20 minutes, until the buns are golden brown and cooked through.

Remove from the oven and cool on a wire rack for about 10 minutes, then drizzle with the sugar glaze.

TO MAKE THE GLAZE

In a small saucepan heat the milk and sugar oven medium heat, stirring constantly with a wooden spoon, until the sugar dissolves and it comes to a slight boil. Reduce the heat to low and simmer for 2-3 minutes.

Note: be sure to watch this carefully as it can boil over or burn very easily.

To serve, gently pull the Chelsea buns apart. They can be served warm or cold. They also freeze well.

SERVINGS: 18

Chelsea Buns
(Bread Machine Method)

The ingredients are the same but if you use a bread machine the job of mixing the dough is a lot easier.

Ingredients

    1 cup milk, room temperature
    1 teaspoon salt
    2 eggs, room temperature
    2 tablespoons butter, softened
    3 cups all purpose flour
    1½ teaspoons yeast
    1½ cups dried mixed fruit, finely chopped
    ½ cup light brown sugar
    ½ teaspoon ground cinnamon
    ⅛ teaspoon ground nutmeg
    ⅛ teaspoon ground ginger
    ⅛ teaspoon ground allspice
    ⅛ teaspoon ground cloves
    ¼ cup butter, melted

Glaze
    ¼ cup superfine sugar
    ¼ cup milk

Method

Place the first six ingredients into the bread machine pan in the order suggested by the bread machine manufacturer. Select the dough cycle and press start.

When the dough is ready, turn it out on a lightly floured surface. Knead lightly until smooth 2 to 3 minutes.

Roll the dough out on a lightly floured surface to form a rectangle approximately 9 inches by 22 inches. Mix together the dried fruit, brown sugar and spices. Brush the dough with the melted butter and sprinkle with the fruit mixture. Roll the dough, from the long side, into a Swiss roll shape and cut into 18 equal pieces using a very sharp knife.

Arrange the buns, cut side down, in a lightly buttered 9 inch x 13 inch baking pan. Lightly brush the tops of the buns with melted butter and cover with plastic wrap. Allow the buns to rise in a warm area for about 30-45 minutes. The buns should be touching each other and the dough will be springy.

Note: the ideal place for the buns to rise is in the oven with just the oven light on.

Before pre-heating the oven, remove the risen buns and, carefully, remove the plastic wrap. Then, pre-heat the oven to 375°F.

Bake at 375°F for about 20 minutes, until the buns are golden brown and cooked through.

Remove from the oven and cool on a wire rack for about 10 minutes, then drizzle with the sugar glaze.

To make the glaze

In a small saucepan heat the milk and sugar oven medium heat, stirring constantly with a wooden spoon, until the sugar dissolves and it comes to a slight boil. Reduce the heat to low and simmer for 2-3 minutes.

To serve, gently pull the Chelsea buns apart. They can be served warm or cold. They also freeze well.

Servings: 18

Victoria Sponge Cake

A slice of Victoria Sponge is often served as one of the choices with high tea. You can also offer a Bakewell Tart, Chelsea Bun or Biscuits.

Ingredients

   1 cup butter, softened
   1½ cups sugar
   4 eggs
   1 teaspoon almond extract
   2 cups all purpose flour
   2½ teaspoons baking powder
   ½ teaspoon salt
   ½ cup raspberry jam
   2 tablespoons confectioners sugar

   Whipped Cream Filling
   ½ pint whipping cream
   1 tablespoon sugar
   ¼ teaspoon real vanilla

Method

Pre-heat the oven to 350°F.

Coat two 8 inch round baking pans with non-stick cooking spray and then flour the baking pans as well.

In a large bowl, cream together the butter and the sugar until light and fluffy. Add the eggs one at a time and beat after each addition. Stir in the almond extract.

In a medium bowl or measuring cup, add the flour, baking powder and salt. Mix well.

Fold in flour mixture into the butter mixture until it is just blended. Do not over mix.

Divide the batter equally between the two prepared baking pans.

Bake the sponge cakes at 350°F for 20 to 25 minutes or until they are golden brown and a wooden toothpick inserted in the center comes out clean.

Allow the cakes to cool completely on a wire rack.

Carefully remove them from the baking pans. Put the first one on a cake plate and spread the top with the raspberry jam.

Whip The Cream

Pour the cream into a pre-chilled bowl that has steep straight sides. Add the sugar and vanilla. Whip with a hand mixer until the cream forms stiff peaks.

Spread the cream on top of the raspberry jam.

Now put the second sponge layer on top and dust the top with the confectioners sugar.

Servings: 12

CRUMPETS

You can't have a book on English baking without a recipe for crumpets but I have to confess this is not something we used to cook ourselves. We just bought them from the local baker. Turns out getting them to look right with the layer of holes on top is kind of tricky.

If you follow the recipe they will taste great but getting them to look right may take a little practice.

INGREDIENTS

3½ cups warm water, divided
1 teaspoon sugar
2 teaspoons active dry yeast
3 cups all purpose flour
1½ teaspoons salt
2 tablespoons powdered whole milk
1 teaspoon baking soda
2 tablespoons warm water

METHOD

In a measuring cup, combine 1 cup of the warm water and the sugar. Mix until the sugar has dissolved in the warm water. Then, sprinkle the 2 teaspoons of active dry yeast on top of the water and set aside in a warm place for about 10 minutes.

The yeast will foam up. If it doesn't, then the yeast is no longer active and you will need to discard it and start again with some active yeast.

In a large bowl, combine the flour, powdered milk and salt. Mix well.

Make a well in the center of the flour mixture and add the yeast water and the rest of the warm water.

Mix well with a fork to make a thick batter.

Cover the bowl with plastic wrap and set aside in a warm place for about an hour to rise. The mixture won't rise a lot but it will expand and get bubbly.

Note: An oven with just the interior light on is a perfect place, and usually warm enough, for the dough to rise.

Once the batter has risen and is nicely bubbly, combine the baking soda with the 2 tablespoons of water and add it to the dough and mix well.

Cover the bowl again with the plastic wrap and let it stand in a warm place for 15 minutes.

Lightly coat a heavy-bottomed frying pan and the crumpet rings (also called English muffin rings or egg rings) with olive oil. It's easiest to do this with a pastry brush. Pre-heat the frying pan and rings together over medium heat.

Note: Getting the temperature just right is a bit of an art. Start with medium heat on your stove and adjust up or down from there based on your results.

When the frying pan and rings are hot, gently put enough dough in each to to come almost to the top of the ring. The dough will rise during cooking.

Cook for 4 to 8 minutes. Bubbles will appear of the entire surface of the crumpet and the dough will start to look dry. At this point, remove the rings and turn the crumpet over. The bottoms should be nicely browned. Cook for an additional 30 seconds to 1 minute to brown the top.

Remove completed crumpets from the pan and cool on a wire rack.

Repeat the process until all the batter is used up.

Crumpets freeze well and can be toasted directly from frozen.

SERVINGS: 24

CRUMPETS (BREAD MACHINE METHOD)

The ingredient quantities are adjusted here to fit most bread machines

INGREDIENTS

- 1 cup water
- 1 tablespoon olive oil
- ¼ teaspoon salt
- 1 tablespoon sugar
- 1 egg
- 2 tablespoons powdered milk
- 1½ cups all purpose flour
- ½ teaspoon baking soda
- 2 teaspoons active dry yeast

METHOD

Place all of the ingredients into the bread machine pan in the order suggested by the bread machine manufacturer. Select the dough cycle and press start.

When the dough cycle is complete, transfer the dough to a large (about 4 cups) measuring cup. Then grease 3 or 4 crumpet rings. Be sure to grease the top and bottom of each ring as well as the inside.

Heat a griddle or heavy skillet over medium heat and grease lightly. Place the crumpet rings on the heated griddle (or skillet) and pour approximately ¼ to ⅓ cup of the dough (depending on the size of your crumpet rings) into each ring.

Note: this is a very sticky, liquid-type of dough that can be difficult to work with.

Cook the crumpets over medium heat until bubbles form on the top and begin to burst. This takes about 8 to 10 minutes. Carefully remove the crumpet rings and turn the crumpets over to brown the other side. This should take 2-3 minutes.

Repeat the process until you have used up all of the dough.

Crumpets freeze well and can be toasted directly from frozen.

SERVINGS: 12

CUSTARD TARTS

If you're familiar with the British TV series "As Time Goes By" starring Judi Dench and Geoffrey Palmer, you'll remember that the Geoffrey Palmer character loved his custard tarts.

INGREDIENTS

    pastry dough, enough for 12 tart shells
    ¼ cup milk
    2 eggs
    1 tablespoon sugar
    ½ teaspoon vanilla
    1 teaspoon nutmeg, freshly ground

METHOD

Pre-heat the oven to 400°F.

On a lightly floured surface, roll out the pastry dough to about ⅛ inch thick and cut out 12 circles. Gently press the pastry circles into muffin tins.

Note: If you are pressed for time, you can use pre-made frozen tart shells (thawed).

Using a whisk, or a fork, beat the eggs, sugar and milk together until well combined. Add the vanilla and stir well.

Pour, or ladle, the egg mixture into tart shells and sprinkle with the freshly grated nutmeg.

Bake the tarts at 400°F for 20 minutes or until custard is set and pastry is cooked through. Remove the tarts from the oven and allow to cool completely on a wire rack.

Variations

Try adding some slices of fresh strawberries, kiwi or peach on top of your tarts.

You can also use this recipe to make one large flan which you decorate with fresh fruit then cut into slices.

Servings: 12

Dundee Cake

Cake and Scotch whiskey - can it get any better?

Ingredients

    1 cup butter, softened
    1⅓ cups packed brown sugar
    4 eggs
    2 cups all purpose flour
    1 teaspoon baking powder
    1 cup raisins
    1 cup currants
    ¾ cup mixed candied peel
    1 tablespoon grated orange peel
    1 tablespoon grated lemon peel
    ¾ cup whole blanched almonds
    2 tablespoons corn syrup
    ½ cup Scotch whiskey

Method

Coat an 8 inch spring-form pan with non-stick cooking spray and set aside.

In a medium bowl, cream together the butter with sugar until light and fluffy.

Add eggs one at a time and beat well after each addition.

In a large bowl, mix together the flour, baking powder, raisins, currants, peel and lemon and orange rinds. Ensure that all of the fruit is well-coated with the flour.

Stir the butter mixture into the flour and fruit mixture and mix until well combined. Pour the batter into the prepared spring-form pan, using a spatula to scrape all of the batter out of the bowl.

Arrange the whole almonds in concentric circles over the entire top of the batter. Then press the almonds lightly into the batter.

Place a loaf pan filled with very hot water in the oven and pre-heat the oven to 300°F.

Bake the cake at 300°F for 2 to 2½ hours or until it is a deep golden color and a wooden toothpick inserted in centre comes out clean.

Allow the cake to cool on a wire rack for 5 minutes before removing it from the spring-form pan. Brush the cake with the corn syrup and then allow it to cool completely on the wire rack.

Soak a large piece of cheesecloth (enough to completely enclose the cake) in half of the whiskey and wrap it around the cake. Brush the cake with the remaining whiskey and wrap tightly in aluminum foil.

Refrigerate the cake for at least a week before serving.

Note: you can refrigerate it for up to a month before serving if you'd like to make it well in advance.

SERVINGS: **14**

English Bath Buns (Bread Machine Method)

Like Chelsea Buns, Bath Buns are made with a yeast dough and have a sweet bread taste.

INGREDIENTS

Dough
½ cup water
½ cup milk
2 eggs
1 teaspoon salt
½ cup butter, softened
2 tablespoons sugar
4 cups all purpose flour
1½ tablespoons active dry yeast

Egg Wash
1 egg, lightly beaten with
1 tablespoon water

Almond Topping
¼ cup sugar
1 cup chopped almonds

METHOD

Place all of the dough ingredients into the bread machine in the order suggested by the bread machine manufacturer. Select the dough setting and press start.

When the dough cycle is complete, transfer the dough to a lightly floured surface and knead slightly.

Divide the dough into 24 equal pieces and shape the pieces into smooth balls then flatten them slightly. Place each flattened ball on a greased cookie sheet and cover with plastic wrap.

Let the buns rise in a warm place for about 30 minutes or until doubled in size.

Note: The best place to let dough rise is in an oven with only the oven light turned on.

Once the buns have risen, remove them from the oven and the pre-heat the oven to 375°F.

While the oven is pre-heating, whisk together the egg and water and brush the tops of the bun with this egg wash.

Note: Don't worry if you have leftover egg wash, you won't need all of it.

Then mix together the chopped almonds and sugar and sprinkle evenly on the buns.

Note: I like to push the chopped almonds slightly into the top of the buns to make sure they'll stick. Just don't push too hard.

Bake the buns at 375°F for 20 minutes or until nicely browned and cooked through. Remove them from the cookie sheet and cool on a wire rack.

SERVINGS: 24

ENGLISH MUFFINS

This is a traditional recipe that makes enough muffins for a large family. If you want less you can freeze the leftovers or look at the bread machine recipe that follows this one.

INGREDIENTS

    1 cup milk
    2 tablespoons sugar
    2 teaspoons active dry yeast
    1 cup warm water
    ¼ cup butter, melted
    6 cups all purpose flour
    1 teaspoon salt
    cornmeal, for coating

METHOD

In a small saucepan, heat the milk over medium-low heat until it comes almost to the boil (small bubble will form). Remove it from the heat and mix in the sugar until it dissolves. Set the saucepan aside and let the milk cool until it is lukewarm.

While the milk is cooling, put the warm water in a small bowl and sprinkle the yeast on top. Let is stand until it is frothy about 10 minutes.

Note: If the yeast does not froth then either the water is too hot or too cold or the yeast is no longer active. In that case, throw out the water/yeast mixture and start again.

In a large bowl combine the milk, yeast mixture, melted butter, 3 cups of the flour and beat until smooth. Then add the salt and the remaining flour. Knead well until the dough is smooth and elastic.

Transfer the dough to a lightly greased bowl. Turn the dough to ensure it is lightly coated in the grease. Cover the dough with plastic wrap and move it to a warm place to rise until doubled in size - about one hour.

Note: The best place to let dough rise is in an oven with only the oven light turned on.

Once the dough has risen, remove the plastic wrap and turn it out onto a lightly floured surface. Punch down the dough and knead slightly. Roll the dough out to about ½ inch thick and cut out rounds with a cookie cutter (about 3 inches in diameter). Sprinkle a baking sheet with cornmeal and place the English muffins on the cornmeal. Then dust the tops of muffins with cornmeal as well. Loosely cover the muffins with plastic wrap and allow to rise for about ½ hour.

Note: The best place to let the muffins rise is in an oven with only the oven light turned on.

Heat a heavy skillet (preferably cast iron) over medium-low heat. Spray lightly with non-stick cooking spray.

Gently squeeze each muffin between your palms, being sure to keep them evenly flat, before placing in the hot skillet so they aren't too "puffy". Cook the muffins in the heavy skillet for about 5 to 7 minutes per side. When you turn the muffins, press down on them evenly with a spatula. The muffins will be golden brown on both sides when they are done.

Note: Squeezing the muffins before putting them in the pan and then pressing on them after you have turned them will help them maintain the traditional English muffin shape

You can split the muffins with a fork or serrated knife while they are still warm and serve immediately, or allow to cool on a wire rack.

These English muffins freeze well and can be thawed and toasted later.

Servings: 24

English Muffins
(Bread Machine Method)

If you're bored with bread and want to try something a little different whip up a batch of English muffins in your bread machine.

Ingredients

>   1 cup milk, room temperature
>   3 tablespoons butter, room temperature
>   1 egg, room temperature
>   ½ teaspoon salt
>   2 teaspoons sugar
>   3 cups all purpose flour
>   1½ teaspoons dry yeast
>   cornmeal, for coating

Method

Place all the ingredients (with the exception of the cornmeal) in the bread machine pan in the order recommended by the manufacturer's instructions.

Select the dough cycle and press start.

When the dough cycle is complete, sprinkle some cornmeal over your work area and remove the dough from the bread machine.

On the prepared surface, pat the dough into a rectangle approximately 1/2 inch thick.

Use your hands to pat the dough into a ½ inch thick rectangle.

Carefully turn the dough so that both sides are lightly coated with the cornmeal.

Using a round cookie cutter (about 3" in diameter), cut out 12 to 14 rounds. Rework any trimmings to get the maximum number of muffins.

Place the English muffins on a baking sheet and cover with plastic wrap. Allow them to rise for about 20-30 minutes or until almost doubled in size.

Heat a heavy skillet (preferably cast iron) over medium-low heat. Spray lightly with non-stick cooking spray.

Gently squeeze each muffin between your palms, being sure to keep them evenly flat, before placing in the hot skillet so they aren't too "puffy". Cook the muffins in the heavy skillet for about 5 to 7 minutes per side. When you turn the muffins, press down on them evenly with a spatula. The muffins will be golden brown on both sides when they are down.

Note: squeezing the muffins before putting them in the pan and then pressing on them after you have turned them will help them maintain the traditional English muffin shape.

You can split the muffins with a fork or serrated knife while they are still warm and serve immediately, or allow to cool on a wire rack.

These English muffins freeze well and can be thawed and toasted later.

SERVINGS: 12

Digestive Biscuits

These traditional British biscuits can be served buttered or with cheese. For a sweeter biscuit, brush one side with melted semisweet chocolate after baking.

Ingredients

¾ cup whole wheat flour
¼ cup all purpose flour
½ teaspoon baking powder
1 tablespoon rolled oats
¼ cup butter
¼ cup brown sugar
¼ cup whole milk

Method

Pre-heat the oven to 350°F and spray a large baking sheet with non-stick cooking spray.

In a large bowl, combine the whole wheat flour, all-purpose flour and baking powder. Mix well. Add in the oatmeal and mix again.

In a small bowl, cream the butter and brown sugar until well mixed.

Add the creamed butter and sugar to the flour mixture and mix well using a fork to make sure the butter mixture gets well incorporated into the flour mixture.

Add the milk and stir until the mixture forms a thick dough.

Knead the dough on a lightly floured surface until smooth, pliable and no longer sticky.

Carefully roll out dough to about ⅛" thick and cut into rounds approximately 2½ inches in diameter with a round cookie cutter.

Note: You may have to re-form any scraps from the first cutting to form the rest of the cookies.

Carefully transfer the biscuits to a greased baking sheet and prick each one well with the tines of a fork.

Note: The biscuits will be fairly fragile so use a very thin spatula to transfer them to the baking sheet.

Bake at 350°F for approximately 22 to 25 minutes, or until an even golden brown.

Remove from the oven and allow to cool completely on a wire rack.

SERVINGS: 14

Hot Cross Buns
(Bread Machine Method)

There are lots of hot cross bun recipes around but to me a hot cross bun has a very distinctive taste and that taste is from cardamom, cloves and nutmeg. I know these are a traditional Easter treat but I have never believed you can't have them anytime of the year.

Maybe I have weird taste buds but I like a piece of old cheddar cheese with my hot cross bun - try it.

Ingredients

Dough

1¼ cups milk, room temperature
2 large eggs
1¾ teaspoons salt
6 tablespoons butter, room temperature
¼ cup light brown sugar, firmly packed
4 cups all purpose flour
½ teaspoon ground cloves
½ teaspoon ground nutmeg
2 teaspoon ground cardamom
1 tablespoon baking powder
1 tablespoon active dry yeast
1½ cups candied mixed peel

Pastry for Crosses
3/4 cup all purpose flour
3 tablespoons cold butter, cut into small pieces
½ tablespoon cold water

Egg Wash
1 large egg
1 tablespoon milk

Glaze
1½ tablespoons apricot jam

METHOD

Add all of the dough ingredients, with the exception of the candied mixed peel, to the bread machine in the order suggested by the manufacturer. Select the dough cycle and press start. Add in the candied mixed peel at the "add-in" beep.

When the dough cycle is complete, transfer the dough to a lightly floured surface and knead slightly. Then divide the dough into 12 equal pieces and shape into balls.

Coat a 9 inch by 13 inch baking dish, preferably glass, with non-stick cooking spray. Place the dough balls in the baking dish, evenly spaced, but not touching. With a very sharp knife, cut a shallow cross into the top of each bun.

Cover the baking dish with plastic wrap and allow buns to rise for about 45 minutes.

Note: The best place to allow dough to rise is in an oven with only the oven light turned on.

MAKING THE PASTRY CROSSES

While the buns are rising it is time to make the pastry crosses.

Cut the butter into the flour until it is well incorporated. Then, add a little cold water (approximately ½ tablespoon) and stir until it makes a thick dough. Add a little more cold water if the dough is too dry.

Roll the dough into a ball and then cut it in half. Cut each half into 6 pieces.

Place the dough in the refrigerator for about 30 minutes. This will make it easier to roll out.

Remove the dough from the refrigerator and roll each piece into a long thin rope. Cut each rope in half and press each piece into the risen buns, forming a cross on the top, being careful not to deflate the buns.

Pre-heat the oven to 350°F.

Making the Egg Wash

Separate the egg white and yolk. Discard the yolk, or put it aside for another recipe. Whisk together the water and egg white until slightly frothy. Brush the tops of the buns with the egg wash.

Bake the buns at 350°F for 20 25 minutes until the are nicely browned.

Remove the buns from the oven and, carefully, transfer them from the baking dish to a wire rack, without separating them. Allow them to cool for about 5 minutes before glazing.

Glazing the Buns

Heat the apricot jam, either on top of the stove or in the microwave, and brush over the still-warm buns to create a nice glaze.

Allow buns to cool completely on a wire rack.

Servings: 12

MADELEINES

OK, what's a sponge cake from North Eastern France doing in a British baking book?

You'd think the name was a dead giveaway that they aren't British but my mother used to make them quite a bit and I never thought to question their origin. At least not until I started to put this book together and looked them up on Wikipedia. So let's just call this a bonus recipe.

You'll need a special Madeleines pan for this recipe which you can find in kitchen specialty shops.

INGREDIENTS

⅓ cup butter
3 eggs
1 cup all purpose flour
½ teaspoon baking powder
⅛ teaspoon salt
⅔ cup sugar
1 teaspoon vanilla extract, real, not artificial
powdered sugar, for dusting

METHOD

Melt the butter and allow it to cool.

With an electric mixer on medium speed, beat the eggs and sugar together until they have approximately tripled in volume. Then add the vanilla extra and beat slightly to incorporate it into the mixture.

In a medium bowl or large measuring cup, mix together the flour, salt and baking powder. Be sure the ingredients are well mixed.

Slowly and carefully fold the flour mixture into the sugar and egg mixture. Be careful not to over mix the batter or it may deflate.

Mix a small amount of the batter into the melted butter. Then slowly fold the butter, about a third of the amount at a time, into the batter. Cover the batter and refrigerate for at least half an hour. The batter should be somewhat firm to the touch.

While the batter is chilling, pre-heat the oven to 375°F. Generously coat the Madeleine tins with non-stick cooking spray and then dust with flour. Shake off any excess flour. It is essential that the pans are well-greased and floured so that the Madeleines will release easily.

Spoon the chilled batter into the prepared Madeleine pans.

Bake at 375°F for 10 to 12 minutes or until the edges are golden brown and the center is slightly springy to the touch. Over-baking will make the Madeleines dry.

Remove the Madeleines from the pans and allow them to cool, smooth side down, on a wire rack. Dust with powdered sugar before serving.

SERVINGS: 24

Maid of Honour Tarts

Ingredients

    12 unbaked tart shells
    3 tablespoons Raspberry or cherry jam
    4 tablespoons butter
    ¼ cup sugar
    1 egg
    ⅓ cup rice flour
    ¼ teaspoon almond flavoring

Method

Pre-heat the oven to 400°F.

Place one teaspoon of jam in each tart shell and set aside.

In a medium bowl, cream the butter and sugar together until light and fluffy. Add the egg and beat the mixture again. Stir in the rice flour and almond flavoring and mix well.

Place a rounded teaspoonful of the mixture in each tart shell.

Bake the tarts at 400°F for about 15 minutes or until pastry and topping are lightly browned.

Remove tarts from the oven and allow them to cool completely on a wire rack.

Servings: 12

Sausage Rolls

Sausage rolls are great as a snack or serve a couple for lunch with some tomato wedges and some Branston™ pickle.

INGREDIENTS

>8 ounces pork breakfast sausage, cooked
>pastry dough, enough for a 1-crust pie

METHOD

Remove the pork breakfast sausages from their package and cook them over medium heat until they are lightly browned.

Remove the sausages to a plate lined with paper towel to absorb any excess fat and allow the cooked sausages to cool to room temperature and cut each sausage in half.

Pre-heat the oven to 400°F.

Roll out the pastry dough and cut it into strips just slightly narrower than the length of the sausages (you want a bit of sausage to peak out at each end), and just long enough to wrap around the sausage with a bit of an overlap.

Wrap the pastry around each sausage half and transfer to a slightly greased baking sheet.

Bake at 400°F. for approximately 10 - 15 minutes or until the pastry is nicely browned.

Remove from oven and cool on a wire rack.

SERVINGS: 24

PASTRY TART SHELLS

Making really good pastry is an art that deserves a book all to itself. As it so happens my wife Vicky makes the best pastry you have ever tasted. Even my mother admitted Vicky's pastry was better than hers.

Lucky for you Vicky has put everything she knows about making pastry into a book called:

"How To Make Perfect Pastry Every Time"

http://ebooks.geezerguides.com/book/how-to-make-perfect-pastry-dough-every-time/

If you're thinking this is just a plug to get you to buy another book, you're wrong - we would like to give you a copy, free of charge.

Just go to http://ebooks.geezerguides.com/register/ and once registered you will get an email whenever we have a free promotion for one of our books.

~~~

INTERNATIONAL MEASUREMENT EQUIVALENTS

This book uses standard US weights and measurements so I have included this chart so you can adjust the recipes to your local system. Equivalents are not exact but close enough for cooking.

DRY MEASURE

Dry measurements are not generally used in US recipes. Only fresh produce such as berries might be measured by the pint. If a US recipe calls for a Pint, Quart or Gallon it is referring to dry measurement which is not the same as liquid measurement.

1 pint, dry = 1.1636 pints, liquid

1 quart, dry = 1.1636 quarts, liquid

1 gallon, dry = 1.1636 gallons, liquid

1 cup, dry = 8 ounces = 16 tablespoon (tbsp)

3/4 cup, dry = 6 ounces = 12 tablespoon (tbsp)

2/3 cup, dry = 5.2 ounces = 10 tablespoon (tbsp) + 2 teaspoons (tsp)

1/2 cup, dry = 4 ounces = 8 tablespoon (tbsp)

1/3 cup, dry = 2.6 ounces = 5 tablespoon (tbsp) + 1 teaspoon (tsp)

1/4 cup, dry = 2 ounces = 4 tablespoon (tbsp)

1/8 cup, dry = 1 ounce = 2 tablespoon (tbsp)

Liquid Measure

Under the US system not only liquids like milk and water use a liquid measurement but other ingredients such as flour, sugar, shortening, butter, and spices are also measured in cups.

Note: The US gallon is larger than the Imperial gallons.

1 gallon (Imperial) = 1.2 Gallon (US) = 4.54 litre

1 teaspoon (tsp) = ⅓ tablespoon (tbsp)
= 1/6 fluid ounce

1 tablespoon (tbsp) = 3 teaspoons (tsp)
= ½ fluid ounce = 1/16 cup

1 fluid ounce = 6 teaspoons (tsp)
= 2 tablespoons (tbsp) = 1/8 cup

1 cup = 48 teaspoons = 16 tablespoons (tbsp)
= 8 fluid ounces = 236 millilitre (ml)

1 pint = 96 teaspoons (tsp) = 32 tablespoons (tbsp)
= 16 fluid ounces = 2 cups = 473 millilitre (ml)

1 quart = 192 teaspoons (tsp) = 64 tablespoons (tbsp)
= 32 fluid ounces = 4 cups = 946 millilitre (ml)

1 gallon (US) = 768 teaspoons (tsp)
= 256 tablespoons (tbsp) =
128 fluid ounces = 8 cups = 3.78 litre

Weight

In the US cooking weights are measured using pounds and ounces. This is the Avoirdupois weight and should not be confused with Troy weight or fluid ounces - which are different.

1 ounce = 28 grams

16 ounces = 1 pound = 454 grams

2.2 pounds = 1 kilogram

TEMPERATURE

In a US kitchen Fahrenheit is all that is required but in Canada both Fahrenheit and Celsius are in use even though Canada officially uses the metric system. Gas Mark is only used in the UK.

250°F = 120°C = Gas Mark ½
275°F = 135°C = Gas Mark 1
300°F = 149°C = Gas Mark 2
325°F = 162°C = Gas Mark 3
350°F = 176°C = Gas Mark 4
375°F = 190°C = Gas Mark 5
400°F = 204°C = Gas Mark 6
425°F = 218°C = Gas Mark 7
450°F = 232°C = Gas Mark 8
475°F = 246°C = Gas Mark 9
500°F = 260°C = Gas Mark 10

Please Review

I hope you have enjoyed this book and will post a favorable review. Independent authors rely on feedback from readers like you to spread the word about books you enjoy. You can leave your comments and contact the author directly by visiting the Amazon web site.

Geezer Guides (the publisher of this book) frequently promotes new titles by offering free copies on special one day only sales. As one of my readers I would like you to get all my new books without charge. Just visit http://ebooks.geezerguides.com and get on their mailing list by filling out the simple form there.

There are many more volumes in this series exploring English cooking from breakfast to dinner and special occasions. Visit http://www.AuthenticEnglishRecipes.com to find out more.

About The Author

Geoff Wells and his wife, Vicky, split their time between Ontario, Canada and the island of Eleuthera in the Bahamas. They maintain several websites including http://www.geezerguides.com which was originally set up for Baby Boomers but has now morphed into the publisher of an eclectic collection of these little booklets.

More information than you could possibly want to know about them is available on their blog

http://www.geoffandvickywells.com

Made in the USA
Columbia, SC
31 July 2017